Marsiyah

Martyrdom of Imam Husayn

Aziz Talbani, Ph.D.

Axis Press

Talbani, Aziz
Marsiyah: Martyrdom of Imam Husayn/ Aziz Talbani
p.cm.
ISBN-13: 978-0692563373
ISBN-10: 0692563377
1. Husayn ibn Ali 2. Islam 3. Karbala 4. Shi'ism 5. Spirituality
Marsiyah: Martyrdom of Imam Husayn

Marsiyah

Martyrdom of Imam Husayn

I'm a clock, tick tock,
I'm time, existed before
> Remain so, eons after

I'm the memory —
> People wish — they forget
> Tyrants wish — they erase
> Clerics attempt — appropriate

This one — memory, history, tragedy
> Changed the nation

Exposed — yet hidden
> Wrapped in faux history

Concealed in reconstituted narratives

Desires draped the creed

Greed swathed politics

You might have heard

Many times before

From countless storytellers

Diverse accounts

Never heard this one before

Truth is revealed, now

Tyrant led people astray

Tyrant —

Silenced voices

Instilled fear

Violated bodies

Blunted minds

Numbed consciousness

Yet the amazing narrative

Survived persecutions, relentless ferocity

To be told

Every moment
Every day

Faction — devout
In their solitude
And in the *majlis*
Venerate the miracle
Live through blessed memories
Nurtured through raptures of souls
Sad convulsions of hearts
A moment in life
Stayed silently — edge of the desert
    Turned into an eternal bliss
    Owe such a moment to Husayn

Today I'll tell, what I saw
On the fateful day,
My inner eye witnessed
    In the heart of desert
    In the heat of the noon
    Scorching sun
Couldn't keep count
Of what was lost
    Scenes of bravery and majesty

Imam, the teacher, the guide, the mystic

Holy bodies — celestial souls
One, two, three,…
They're not numbers
Many into one —
Cosmic souls — Encompass all
    Bodies and souls
    Symbols and meanings
    Patient and persevering
    And lingering hope for *Umma*

Time passed — reckoning begins
    Who has the register —
    Who keeps records?
What was lost?
A story, a memory, faith or truth
Never found in books
Or consciousness of people

Truth lost, drop by drop — drip drop
    When all was over
    At the dusk, red horizon
    Burning amber was the caravan

Martyrs heads carried on spears
Silhouettes of women and children
Marching at a distance —
Heads uncovered, empty hands, bare feet
Surrounded by hapless soldiers —
Without consciousness or
A shred of conscience
Flock of sheep — repeat tall tales
    Pointing spears and swords
    Still scared of power —
    Of women and children

Women's stories that live on
    Not an ordinary family
    Caliber unmatched
    The family of Muhammad[sa]

The noblest of all, Mustafa[sa] wept
    Had a vision —
    few decades after him
    His family decimated
Allah had given signs
The holy book warned

It all began after the last Hajj
It wasn't an easy charge —
Challenge greater than fighting infidels
Burden heftier than the year of sorrow

The Prophet —
    Allah's beloved *Rasul*
    Most intimate friend
    Didn't announce at Arafat

Yet Allah warned him —
Mission is not done
The message must be delivered
"Allah will protect thee from people"
    Who are the people?
    Think — people?
    Lend your ears
Open the window to your consciousness
I'll let you in on the secret —
Some were present and others were yet to come

At Ghadir — another stop
Remember the meaning of faith

Presence of Allah in your life

Remember the hereafter

Never forget the Prophet's nobility

    — Intercessor and guide

In the world and hereafter

Manifest Truth

Among the believers

"One who saw me has witnessed the Truth"

The Prophet proclaimed

And extending it to Ali —

Nearest to Allah and Mustafa

    — Is Murtaza

Now "Ali is

 Lord over you"

The only link

To the meaning of faith

The only guide

To *Qiyamah*

Rasūl Allah proclaimed

"Ali — custodian of knowledge

The meaning of the book revealed

Through Ali and my progeny"

Walaya completed Islam

Concluded its last principle
Ali the source for *marifah*
Guidance to the truth
And *mushkil kusha*
His hand always extends
To you; in all times
The Prophet's mercy present
Through Ali
Left the Prophet — clear guidance
Thus Allah completed Islam

Yet many paths opened up
　　Some believed in a state —
　　Others creed, doctrines, rituals
　　Few and only few
　　Followed the baraka and noor
Of Ali and his kin

Eventually —
Monarchy took over
Nabi warned at Arafat
Avarice is Satan
Greed is stagnation
Don't let it take over —

Your lives — losing bet
A perilous deal
Alas! Oblivious; paid no heed

Enlightened people of Safa
    Saw ominous signs
    Sobbed for times to come
With insight in
Ahmed's wisdom — knew
A new struggle is to begin
This time —
    For the soul of Islam
    To preserve it, carry it
    and live it

Some sixty years after an-Nabi
The grandson Husayn ibn Ali
Brings the family with him —
Was it a journey for the kingdom?
    Or wealth
    Or power
    Nay!

It was a unique journey

With the blessed family
No ordinary kin
Angels bow to them
Jinns follow their command
Dead and alive; people
Seek their mercy
When facing calamities
In life; hunger, disease, disaster
When taking the last breath
Facing inquisition in the grave
At the bridge to eternity
Stern moment in *Qiyamah*
 Fate to be decided
The family of the Prophet
Extends the mantle of grace

It was the journey taken by the Imam
 Awakened consciousness
 Enlightened mind; bearer of Noor
 Custodian of Prophet's wisdom
Revealing the path to be *abd*
Ahmed's intimacy with Ahad
 The essence of *mi'raj*

Husayn now walks the track
　　The path for all —
Man, woman, and child
Husayn rides Zuljannah
　　Buraq's earthly reflection
The caravan departs Mecca

Husayn waits for people to join
Few moments of silence
Bows his head in reflection
Remembers days he played with grandpa
Climbing on his shoulder during prayers
Sitting on his lap through sermons
Or hugs while playing in streets

Then Husayn raises his head, looks behind
No Meccan joined him
Fear blocked their path
Or greed hindered their way
Or lack of consciousness?

Takes a deep sigh
Recognizes — the time has not yet come
For them

To take the journey

The journey is of choice and love
    Love and choice, not given
Nurtured in hearts and minds
The journey not an easy one
For those whose hearts have
    Wisdom of Mustafa
    Purity of purpose
    Zikr of Almighty
    It's a spiritual toil
Takes a lot
Total submission
Like the sacrificial lamb

The journey is a metaphor
For *mi'raj*
Fana in Allah
For mind —
    Enter the gate of knowledge
    Emancipate from worldly delusions
    Open to possibilities
To witness the signs
    In the self, horizon and cosmos

Clean the heart —

    Without biases and prejudices

    Fill with respect and kindness

    Generosity and service

Soul —

   Recipient of bliss and noor

Husayn meditates; it may take generations

Centuries to unfold

The meaning of this journey

Truth sought by few

Not a majority/minority contest

Not an easy path

The caravan must go

Husayn nudges Zuljannah

On the way — Hurr stops

No passage to Kufa

Hurr out of water

Imam gives water

    Soldiers and horses all

Hurr diverts them to Karbala

    Barren desert, wilderness

Thousands more soldiers

surround them

harass them

Euphrates blocked

Desert heat reaches zenith

Man, woman, and child

Thirsty and famished

Abbas ibn Ali

With a water bag

Rides to Euphrates

His journey to eternity begins

Shower of arrows

Unsheathed swords

Receive him pointing spears

Undeterred by the offensive

He cuts through soldiers

Secures water

Fights back —

Soldiers surround him

One arm is slashed — blood flows

Holds in the other arm

The other arm cut

Pain excruciating —

Holds the water bag

In the mouth

Rushes to the camp

Body covered with arrows

Swords' wounds

Bravely endures pain

Mind focused on the Imam

Must reach the camp

Woman and child, old and young

Thirsty, thirsty, …

His parched lips — feel wet

Blood dripping from the head

Covers the face

Saddle soaked, ride drenched

He falls — eyes fixed on the camp

Pictures children, women, and sick

And his Imam

"Ya Mawla

I am sorry

Didn't bring water"

Hears his Imam's words

"Abbas — mercy on you

Go meet our beloved Prophet

And father and mother

They're witnessing
The unfolding
Of history's chapter"

The Prophet's family — without water
Alas, it wasn't just water
It exposed — people without compassion
People filled with hate and greed
People steeped in the oblivious
The *Umma* will remain thirsty —
For eons to come —
For grace and bliss
Only those'll receive
With knowledge from *ahl-al bayt*

Abbas looks up
Descending from heaven
Solemn troops of angels – Tears rolling
— to receive Abbas
Silence prevails
Abbas in eternal peace
Departs with Imam's blessings

Like wolves and vultures

Rushing to their prey

Encircled

    Naked swords

    Pointing spears

    Showering arrows

Thousands

All toward the small ensemble

Family of the Prophet

and few companions

Nothing shakes consciousness

    Or rids the blind folds

    Or opens their hearts

Neither the holy lineage

Nor the sight of

    Women, children, and sick

Is the army — made of stone? or

    Clay from the bottom of hell

    Muck from the deep well of ignorance

    Smut from the recess of wickedness

    Or from the ocean of ignominy

Are they soldiers?

Or thugs preying on women, children and sick

Or mercenaries seeking loot

The Imam reflects —

Looks at the encircling army

    Swords shimmering in sun

    Pointing spears shining at noon

    Drum beating with haunting sound

Imam goes to the tent

The last ditch effort

To shake up their conscience

Remove blindfolds — from their souls

Awaken their spirit

Show them the path

Brings Ali Asghar

A baby – thirsty, crying

A baby going through

    Trauma of war

    Subject to hate

    Suffering agony

Face flushed red in heat

Tiny arms wavering

As if praying to an intimate God

Or trying to hold the invisible hand

Or impatient to meet the divine

Imam raised Ali Asghar
"Oh people, look
He's a baby
Whose water you blocked
A baby whose life you halt
    Do you know who Ali Asghar is?
    His tears will drown the ocean
    His cry is the bugle of Israfel
    and his sight is the vision of Gabriel
    Beware — don't be led by greed
    For reward or power —
    In his life
     is life hidden for you
    In his voice
     is consciousness for you
    Preserve him
     and you'll live forever."

People made of greed
 Ignorance or hate; who knows?
What caused their blindness?
 Or their motives

For this pathetic bet
Give up the eternal life;
 For scraps of the world
Forsake the bliss of Prophet;
For the slavery of a tyrant

Heat, humidity, and swirling high sand jinn
Resounding war drums and
Swooshing arrows
Responding to Imam's counsel
With showers of arrows and spears
An arrow pierces —Ali Asghar

The body — like a flower
Fragile as a glass
Like a glittering star
Light spreads through the lamp
As darkness overtakes
Desert noon

Now darkness casts over —
The hearts and minds
What they believe or know
All futile, all in vain,

Ali Asghar is silent —

His silence – penetrates the recess of

    Heavens and earth

Pierces through the hearts of

Angels and jinns

Prophets and saints — bow their heads

In shame— people could be so cruel

In grief — pain could be so deep

Imam holds the tiny body

In his arms — blood

    Hands covered

    Robe soaked

    And Imam's heart…?

Desert – thirsty

Takes one more life

    Blood recedes into sand

Karbala never seen such deep darkness — at noon

Darkness of minds and souls

Sorrow engulfs — Imam's heart

The people lost their way — So soon …

Forgetting favors the Prophet did —
Brought them from darkness to light
Yet, all seems lost—

Returning to the age of ignorance
    Worshiping again idols
    Of Monarchy
    Dogma
    Material indulgence

The Imam returns to the tent
Prepares for the final bout—
Few go against thousands
It's not one battle — its multitudes
 Layers up layers
 Fought on many grounds
 Innumerable times
 At multiple levels
Of consciousness
 For the meaning of faith
 Purpose of *Din*

Those who deny Husayn now
 Their progenies will fight;

For eons to redeem

Those who'll follow Husayn

Their progeny exert to stay on the path;

Face persecution, disapproval, condemnation

Those who remain perplexed

Will toil to take the journey

Husayn's journey remains the passage to truth

This journey

    Is not about numbers

    Or rational choice made for plunder

    Or saving earthly life

It is the battle where —

    Wisdom goes against ignorance

    Noor against darkness

    Conscience against apathy

    Consciousness against oblivion

    Islam against monarchy

That's where Husayn stands

Hurr sees the evil side

Fighting against the truth

Bows his head in shame

He counsels with few and decides

Galloping to the Imam
Bows to him
"Ya Mawla, have mercy
My life and services
At your feet."
Mawla blesses him
"Hurr go, receive eternal freedom"

Husayn's loyal few
One by one — they fight
One by one
Comrades martyred —
Witnessing the truth
Partaking heaven's nectar
Quenching the thirst of lifetime
Escorting angels — envious of
Companionship they had with the Imam
Blessed life — revered death — sublime hereafter

Husayn — alone in the battlefield
Eerie silence prevails
Encircling army — ready
Shooting arrows
Aiming spears

Pointing swords

The moment has arrived
Divine light shines through Husayn
Apprehensive angels — encircle horizon
Awaiting Husayn to say the word
 A curse, a condemnation, or a command
"We'll turn that army to ashes —
Their arms into melting liquid
Fear we'll instill in their hearts
They'll crawl into mothers' bosom
Like Abrah's soldiers
Ate the dust — those survived
Ran fast — to their shelters"

Husayn stays patient — lips utter prayers
Calamity facing, yet follows
Grandfather's path — peace and forgiveness
The sky illuminates
Bliss descends on him

Husayn moves forward
The enemy retreats
Scared to fight — keeps the distance

Shooting arrows and throwing spears

A spear penetrates Imam's chest
Blood gushes
Wound is deep
Yet Husayn is calm
Bears the pain
 Imam is serene
Fights back
Arrows and more arrows
Spears and more spears
Imam's holy body
Covered with wounds
Flowing blood
He fights – his body takes wounds
 Uncounted
  Blood covers saddle

Zuljannah sees the master's wounds — tears flow
Stomps the ground
    with anger
    with disgust
Wished he could squash low life
    Dumb, deaf, and blind

Armies of ignorance

Worshiping mundane desires

The moment,

Husayn prostrates to offer

The last *sajda*,

Transcends all acts of worship;

All times to come

Husayn's sacrifice, the sublime

He is *abd*

As he closes to the ground

Distance diminishes between

Abd and *ma'bood*

Reaches the stage — where

Two become one

Shemr — the cursed one

Separates head from body

Sealing the fate of people

Live in oblivion

Die in ignorance

Grace doesn't touch their souls

Marcy enters not their hearts

Darkness spreads

Inside and out
They loot, burn and desecrate

The Prophet's family
Women brave and dignified
Stood firm
Bear the pain
Hold back their tears
Hide their grief
Stand up against tyranny

No submission to a tyrant
Silently walk the desert
The road to Damascus
City of sorrow,
Swallowed great empires
Waiting to nip another

Armies of scribes hired
Rewrite the history
Seize people's thoughts
Capture their souls' desires
Ignoble Judges sleep peacefully —

Tomorrow to write another fiction — for a
nefarious master
Elite enjoy wine and music in harem — celebrate

Vanquishing speaker of truth — darkness has
spread
Hiding the true Master
Silence is imposed —
Concealing the calamity of the martyrdom
People dreaming in their shacks — fed with
illusions

Fictions of bygone glories
Buildings erected to cement fame
On people —
Consciousness as if never dawned
Conscience, never nurtured
In people

The age of ignorance rises again
From the desert — with the sword of a tyrant
Darkness devoured the legend
of Husayn — they thought!

As sun rises the day after

Images disappear — the desert returns to cruel
loneliness

An army of writers gather

To spin new stories

Theologian conjecture futile worldly problems

Starving laborers wander in bazaars to fill their
bellies

Gangs of police walk through streets

Their specter — creates fear

    Presence of cataclysm

    Sense of impending disaster

    Violence and mistrust become the norm

    Humans reduced to —

        Incarnates of animal instincts

Who's eavesdropping, who's spying,

Who's friend and who's a foe?

Tyrant paranoid, afraid,

So are the people

Society shapes sans

Trust, mercy, happiness

 Refuge in delusions

The day after — new stories were woven
Conscience of a people silenced
Consciousness numbed
The family imprisoned

The battle was fought in a day
But truth was stolen behind veils
Meanings appropriated
By conspiracies in palace chambers
In corridors of seminaries
Behind closed doors of jurists

The thief came, took the meaning away
The battle for meaning and symbols
No one knew — fought
But who won, who lost
It wasn't for the throne and sword
It was for the healing of the soul
 Of community

Alas! People comfortable in their slumber
Some watched through night vigils
How dark shadows pass through souls —

Souls of heedless

The Prophet's words prevailed

"Islam grew in exile, will return to it"

New rules, altered beliefs, monarchy

Jahiliya wine in new bottles

Ulama write new creeds

Writers and artist — prosper — attending elites

Sword rules — tribal accounts

Some wonder what happened

That fateful day — when all changed

No one knew

The Story teller

Sits in a corner of the bazaar

Rubbing his head in anxiety

Exuberating confusion

Something is stolen from my stories

Meaning of words — changed

Words, symbols

He cries in silence

Holds back his tears

Police stand close by

Spies are in the crowd

Streets of Damascus, Mecca, Medina
And distant towns — bleeding hearts
Voices are exiled
Thoughts curtailed
Truth like air can't capture in a fist

Tyrant's religion — Obey the ruler
   Follow his commands
   Don't ask questions
Tyrant's religion
   A new industry of violence
   In many forms/shapes
   Fear/punishment;
   Mental/physical/spiritual
    Conquests/destruction — dismemberment
    People/places — cultures
    Violence and fear here/hereafter
Tyrant's religion — hedonism
Harem/wine/pleasures
Tyrant's religion
Creates labels, new narratives, and noise
What could not be erased —
Appropriate, change, modify — confuse

New language, new era

Heretics, infidels, separatists, foreigners

Loathe them, fear them, and destroy them

Is the recurring message

Registered in the consciousness of people

Destroyers of ancestral culture

A new narrative of fear

Mistrust, antagonism

We and they

Ours and theirs

Monopoly over truth — sword decides

Mobs run amuck —   kill those who disagree

Kill those who love *Ahl al-Bayt*, or

Write, talk, or remember them

Thousands murdered, imprisoned, tortured

So they thought — annihilated Shia

Consciousness of people — diminished

So does the consciousness of nation

Ideas, thinkers, writers, philosophers

The secret that the Prophet told

That tongue is silenced

So they thought!

Voices of wisdom
Secrets awaken in the soul
Mantle of grace remains
Husayn's wounds — a community's wounds
A community evolves with unhealed wounds
Tensions and scars remain

The Community
Never realizing what was lost
What was stolen?
Never recognizing who were thieves
A drunken, corrupt tyrant wasn't alone
Often the power of fiction
Hides more than that it reveals
Truth is covered in thousand veils

Those who insist — let swords decide, unaware
Our Lord Husayn's martyrdom
Sign of end times; coming
Beginning of the end

Petty tyrants, swarm like reptiles;

Besiege the sacred, holy in life
On the hallow grounds of truth

Violated by the muck, people covered in
Shining robes, gold in fingers and necks
Ran amok goons of devil
    Armies of tyrant
In so many guises — men of faith
Scholars, merchant in bazaar,
Jesters in street, or writers
They march through our consciousness
Penetrate in our minds
With fib they torment our souls
Put us on the path of confusion

Is the Prophet's mantle gone?
Is meaning lost forever?
Faith just regurgitation, routine or
 Numbing repetition

Fairytale history — replaced wisdom of the family
Gloom of dark souls — ousted the joy of spirits
Hatred/distrust —
Violence of uncontrolled anger — prevails

Confusion and despondency
Who would know?

Tyranny of power destroys itself
Rendering mayhem
    starving minds and souls
Pulpits, preachers, penchants
Diatribe — men's words envelope God's
Rulers' service blends with God's
Follow the wealthy/powerful
Rulers serve pitcher/goblet
Song/music/devious words
Time lost in drinks
Company of dancers, jesters, sycophants
What do they know?
Game in the world — zero sum
Gained nothing, preserved nothing

Journey of a soul in the dark
From darkness to darkness
From absurdity of man-made beliefs
    to loneliness of eternally damned
Tyranny drives strength from division
    Legitimacy from violence

Its sustenance — from sycophants

Vicious circles of events
Counting bodies each day
And beginning again the next
Insolent to
      Tears and fears of a mother,
      Sigh of a father
      Sobbing of brothers/sisters/bride

History of the followers of tyranny
      Believe without certitude
      Know nothing
      Explore none
      Delusions in mind
      Doubts in heart
      Darken their world
      Rituals, routines, dogma

Their destiny
      Live in anger
      Die in despair
Without knowing
      What the Prophet brought?

Why Husayn shed his blood?

Why their conscience silent?

Why their consciousness in the dark?

Where they lost the path?

Why they adhere to tyrants?

Reverberate memories of women/children

Disappearing in the desert sunset

Husayn's blood absorbed in desert sand

Emerges from the dunes

Perfumes the ether of life

From Husayn's heart to

The core of humanity's soul

In distance places — thought ferments

Who knew?

Where voices and promises of victims' silences

 Blossom, a new language

Words, meanings, the Prophet's grace

Remained through Husayn's blood

Who knew?

When the sounds of battle drums stopped

In exile — new stories are told

Struggle begin anew
A fraction comes out from shadows
Kindle the love of Husayn
Spread the wisdom of *Ahl al-Bayt*

A doctor's clinic
A bookseller's library
A sufi's cloister
Books exchanged stealthily
Messages delivered covertly
All in silence, hidden, preserving meaning
Meeting in secret for wisdom and science
But for the few

Centuries after centuries
The Prophet's promise fulfilled
Light upon light,
In hearts, minds, and verily
Through words, pens, and brushes

Light embraces
In despair, in struggle, poverty
In riches too
A ray of light shines

Engulfs

Guides

Holds your hand

Always, always keeps you

Closer to the source

Prophet said

"Islam grew in exile, will return to it"

Oh Lord Husayn, I submit to thee

Rescue us from fables of unholy

Free myself, free my mind, my soul

Yazids of the time though powerful

Your bliss, a drop of it, enough

To heal the wounded soul

Relieve the pain

And shatter the darkness

Let vanish

Long cast shadow of doubt

Reclaim the mantle of protection

Please protect — what's sacred in us

Relieve us from pain,

invisible and unspoken

Protect the bosom custodian of thy story

The miracle that's Husayn's story

The story of truth and love

Husayn left, never gone
His light shines
At mid-night vigils
Early morning zikr
Day time toil
Discerning Zulfiqar — shreds ignorance
Zuljannah swift through life — discovering
    Open thy mind,
     Window to thy spirit
What you need in life
You'll have it
Let open your heart and
Light of Husayn brings eternal peace
Right now — right here
Open the door,
Or a window
Or even a key hole to your soul
His light will cover your
Existence — give yourself a chance
No one returns empty handed
    from the threshold of Mustafa
His touch transforms

Revives the dead

Give riches beyond imagination

Husayn's voice echoes

In consciousness of mine

Sleep walk through life

The death you escape has occurred

The battle you fight against tyranny

Awakens thyself with nightly vigils

Wraps around with love a lonely heart

That evening, travelers

Stranded in a desert

Burning tents, sobbing kids

A deep wound in memory

The memory of martyrs

When in his *majlis*

In your tears

Aches in your hearts

Rest assured — Husayn is present

Hold him — in your arms

Hold him — in your eyes

Hold him — in your heart

And from your consciousness

Never, ever let the Iman go…

The Author

Dr. Aziz Talbani was awarded PhD and MA degrees from McGill University, MA from the University of London, and MA from Karachi University. He has taught and spoken at Institutions of Higher Education in North America, Europe, and Asia. As a faculty member, he taught in Educational Leadership and Teacher Education programs. His primary specialization is in areas of diversity and cultural competency. Through the decades, Aziz has mentored many students in diverse fields including Education and Religious Studies. He notes, "My most rewarding experiences come from working with communities in various parts of the world on social justice and equity issues, educational development, and women's rights." As a writer and artist, his current focus is on fiction writing including novels, short stories, and poetry.

Forthcoming Books:

Muhammad[sa] in Ismaili Gnosis: History, Philosophy, and Spirituality, 2016.

Source Book on Diversity: Post-Modern Analysis, 2016.

A Manual for Diversity Training, 2016.

Life on the Dark Side of the Moon (Fiction).

www.ingramcontent.com/pod-product-compliance
Lightning Source LLC
Chambersburg PA
CBHW071352130626
46556CB00005B/2152